HOW
PROPHETS
FAIL

by Jonas Clark

Unless otherwise noted, Scripture quotations are taken from the King James Version.

HOW PROPHETS FAIL
ISBN-10: 1-886885-43-5
ISBN-13: 978-1-886885-43-1

Copyright © 2010 by Jonas Clark

Published by Jonas Clark Ministries
27 West Hallandale Beach Blvd.
Hallandale, Florida, 33009-5437, U.S.A.
(954) 456-4420

www.JonasClark.com

HOW PROPHETS FAIL

Not every prophet makes it. Some turn to the dark side. Satan has nothing to work with except what's already in you. His strategy has never changed. He entices through the lust of the eyes, the pride of life and the deceitfulness of riches. Prophetic ministers must avoid the seducing pull of wealth, honor, prestige and promotion. These are all tempting assignments used to corrupt God's true prophets.

The story of Balaam is a great lesson for every emerging prophet. He started off right in his ministry but something went terribly wrong. The enemy introduced a barrage of demonic enticements against him targeting the hidden idolatry deep within the recesses of his heart. The assignments worked. Balaam didn't make it and lost his ministry and his life. This could happen to you too.

Balaam was a true prophet that erred because of the idolatry in his own heart. This is how it happened. The people of Moab were the children and the offspring of Lot and his daughter. They were an incestuous tribe. The Israelites terrified King Balak and he was overcome with dread when he heard they were near. Acting out of he sent messengers to God's prophet, Balaam, who lived in Pethor, 320 miles north of Moabite country near Haran. Abraham also lived in Haran, and you recall that Abraham left that heathen land later to become the man that God called His friend.

number
6-7 "Come now therefore, I pray thee, curse me this people; for they are too mighty for me: peradventure I shall prevail, that we may smite them, and that I may drive them out of the land: for I know that he whom thou blessest is blessed, and he whom thou cursest is cursed. And the elders of Moab and the elders of Midian departed with the rewards of divination in their hand; and they came to Balaam, and spake to him the words of Balak." (Numbers 22:6-7)

The elders of Moab tempted Balaam with rewards, money for divination and money for curses. They were there to buy the prophet's prophetic services. Was Balaam's ministry known to be for sale? What about yours? "Never," you say. Are you sure? Is there anything for the devil to work with buried deep within you? If there is he will find it.

> "And he (Balaam) said to them, Lodge here this night, and I will bring you word again, as the Lord shall speak to me: and the princes of Moab abode with Balaam." (Numbers 22:8)

Balaam asked these elders to spend the night that he might bring word as the Lord may speak. The word "Lord" here means Jehovah. If you have any wonder about whom this prophet served, he was inquiring of Jehovah God. This would confirm that Balaam was a true prophet of God. "And God came to Balaam, and said, What men are these with thee?" (Numbers 22:9) Do you think God knew who these men were? The answer is obvious of course. So then, God must have had a reason for asking Balaam who these men were. Let's read on.

"And Balaam said to God, Balak the son of Zippor, king of Moab, hath sent to me, saying, Behold, there is a people come out of Egypt, which covereth the face of the earth: come now, curse me them; peradventure I shall be able to overcome them, and drive them out. And God said to Balaam, Thou shalt not go with them; thou shalt not curse the people: for they are blessed." (Numbers 22:10-12 Italics added)

Before we can go any further we must make something clear. Did God say that Balaam could go with them? The answer is absolutely not. God said that Balaam could not go with them nor curse the people He had blessed. We need to make sure that we are clear on this point because later God is going to let Balaam go and we want to learn why.

"And Balaam rose up in the morning, and
said to the princes of Balak, Get you into
your land: for the Lord refuseth to give me
leave to go with you." (Numbers 22:13)

The next morning Balaam told the princes of Balak
to go back home because Jehovah refused to allow him
to go with them. Isn't it interesting that Balaam did
not tell the Moabites the rest of what God told him?
He failed to mention the blessing on these people and
to curse them would not be possible.

"And the princes of Moab rose up, and they
went to Balak, and said, Balaam refuseth
to come with us." (Numbers 22:14)

So the princes of Moab went back and told King
Balak that Balaam the prophet refused to come with
them. These princes did not tell the king the whole
story either. They should have told the King that

Jehovah God would not allow the prophet Balaam to come. These communications got progressively worse by leaving bits of the Word of the Lord out of the discussions. King Balak didn't know what was going on. He couldn't understand why the prophet wouldn't come. He thought that perhaps he hadn't offered him enough money. Now if the princes of Balak would have come back with the Word of the Lord saying, "Thou shalt not go. You can't curse blessed people," then perhaps King Balak would have turned from his wicked ways.

HIGH LEVEL ENTICEMENTS

Balak was persistent. He thought Balaam was just holding out for more money. King Balak was ready to negotiate. Scripture says,

> "And Balak sent yet again princes, more,
> and more honorable than they. And they

came to Balaam, and said to him, Thus saith Balak the son of Zippor, Let nothing, I pray thee, hinder thee from coming to me: For I will promote thee to very great honor, and I will do whatsoever thou sayest to me: come therefore, I pray thee, curse me this people." (Numbers 22:15-17)

"For I will promote thee." Can you see the demonic p-u-l-l of these assignments against this prophet of God? The king's most honorable representatives (high-level demonic ambassadors) used the lust for power, honor, money, prestige, enticements with smooth flattering sayings to entice Balaam. These are all high-level demonic enticements designed to pull on any common ground that might be in the heart of God's prophet. You will face the same assignments. Your enemy is a master in the art of seduction. Before you can be deceived he has to flatter you first. Remember your prophetic ministry comes from Christ. No man, demon or angel can promote you. Never forget that.

> "And Balaam answered and said to the servants of Balak, If Balak would give me his house full of silver and gold, I cannot go beyond the word of the Lord my God, to do less or more." (Numbers 22:18)

Doesn't this sound honorable coming from the prophet Balaam? This is a good answer, yet he should also have reminded the delegation what the Lord said to him the first time. He should have said, "I don't know why you're wasting your time. God said that He would not let me curse a blessed people." Let's read what the prophet did.

> "Now therefore, I pray you, tarry ye also here this night, that I may know

what the Lord will say to me more."
(Numbers 22:19)

This was Balaam's second mistake. God had already spoken to him saying, "Thou shalt not go with them; you shall not curse the people, for they are blessed." Yet Balaam spoke to God about it again.

> "And God came to Balaam at night, and said to him, If the men come to call thee, rise up, and go with them; but yet the word which I shall say to thee, that shalt thou do." (Numbers 22:20)

Did God change His mind? Why would God tell Balaam not to go and then tell him to go? Was God answering Balaam according to the idolatry in his heart? Is it dangerous to keep pressing God in prayer after he has already spoken? Were these demonic lures still seeking common ground in Balaam's heart? Why did God change his mind? Let's look for the answer in the prophetic life of Ezekiel.

> "Son of man, these men have set up their idols in their heart and put the stumbling block of their iniquity before their face: should I be inquired of at all by them?" (Ezekiel 14:3)

What does it mean to put the "stumbling block of their iniquity before their faces?" Like we have already discussed, stumbling blocks are idols in a person's life that are more important to them than God. These men that approached Ezekiel were asking God to bless their idols. Balaam was such a man. He had it in his heart to go. He continued to press God for permission even after God told him not to go. Balaam's ministry could be bought. The demonic assignment was working. The hook was set. The prey captured. Balaam was crossing the threshold. This is a warning for you. Don't keep asking God to allow you to do something when He has already said no. Don't forget that God is watching you, trying the reigns of your heart and proving your faithfulness.

BLESS MY IDOLS

Idols are dangerous and deadly. God opposes anything that separates him from his children. Idols are anything that separates you from God. If God asked you to do something for him, but there was always something else that you had to do first, then that could be idolatry. Whatever it is that consistently pulls you away from the Father is idolatry. The real insult to God is when one asks God to bless their stumbling blocks of idolatry.

Modern man may not bow down to wooden idols yet there are many other idols. Idolatry is anything that pulls you away from God. Idols might be a man, woman, job, house, car, children, money, television, sports, hobbies, animals or even your ministry. Whatever it is that separates your heart from an intimate relationship with Jesus, is idolatry. Idols can represent lust in your heart the enemy can use to pull on you, like idols of self-will. Some say "God blesses the work of your hands," but if the work of your hands pulls you away from God, it is not blessings from God.

The demonic enticements against Balaam were designed to find any idols in his heart the enemy could use to separate him from God. Prophets must guard themselves against these same demonic assignments.

> "Therefore speak to them, and say to them, Thus saith the Lord God; Every man of the house of Israel that setteth up his idols in his heart, and putteth the stumbling block

of his iniquity before his face, and cometh to the prophet; I the Lord will answer him that cometh according to the multitude of his idols." (Ezekiel 14:4)

There are many people asking God to bless their idolatry even after God has already said no. Because of their persistence there is a danger that God will answer them according to the multitudes of their idolatry. In other words, it may appear that God is changing his mind by telling them only what they want to hear.

BALAAM'S IDOLATRY

Let's look again at what the prophet Balaam did. Remember God clearly said, "Thou shalt not go," then he told Balaam to go.

"And God came to Balaam at night, and said to him, If the men come to call thee, rise up, and go with them; but yet the word which I shall say to thee, that shalt thou do." (Numbers 22:20)

God looks at your heart to see what is in there (Psalm 7:9). Balaam was ready and eager to go with the Moabites. God had already spoken to Balaam saying that he could not go. Did God change his mind? Not really, but God tested the prophet to see what was in his heart. With God's permission Balaam saddled up his donkey and set out for Moab country. Scripture says, "And God's anger was kindled because he went: and the angel of the Lord stood in the way for an adversary against him. Now he was riding upon his ass, and his two servants were with him." (Numbers 22:22) God was angry with Balaam.

Some ask, "But God, you said that he could go." True, but that did not mean that Balaam was supposed to go. Can you see this? God had answered Balaam according to the idolatry in his heart because Balaam had continued to press God in prayer.

God may do that to us too. God might say, "Well, if you want to do that, even after I have already said no, then go ahead." You had better watch out though, you could be entering a test. Some people ask, "Where is that scripture that says that God will give you the desires of your heart?" I tell them, "Right here!" (Ezekiel 14:4). God will give you the desires of your heart to prove and to test you, but what if the wants of your heart are not right? It is always important that we examine our motives.

BALAAM'S HEART

God was angry with the prophet Balaam "because he went." Let's read what happened to Balaam on the way to Moabite territory.

"And the ass saw the angel of the Lord standing in the way, and his sword drawn in his hand: and the ass turned aside out of the way, and went into the field: and Balaam smote the ass, to turn her into the way. But the angel of the Lord stood in a path of the vineyards, a wall being on this side, and a wall on that side. And when the ass saw the angel of the Lord, she thrust herself unto the wall, and crushed Balaam's foot against the wall: and he smote her again. And the angel of the Lord went further, and stood in a narrow place, where was no way to turn either to the right hand or to the left. And when the ass saw the angel of the Lord, she fell down under Balaam: and Balaam's anger was kindled, and he smote the ass with a staff." (Numbers 22:23-27)

Balaam's anger was kindled because he was being delayed and he struck his donkey. Notice the anger in the prophet's heart? Nothing was going to get in Balaam's way. Nothing was going to stop him from his pursuit, not even a faithful donkey. Idolatry is an evil thing.

> "And the Lord opened the mouth of the ass, and she said unto Balaam, What have I done unto thee, that thou hast smitten me these three times? And Balaam said unto the ass, because thou hast mocked me: I would there were a sword in mine hand, for now would I kill thee." (Numbers 22:28-29)

The way Balaam responded to his animal revealed a deep-seated anger in his life. He was full of murder and self-will. A murderous, self-will spirit was in the heart of this prophet. Nothing would keep him from the idolatry in his heart. He was even ready to kill his own faithful donkey. Anger and murder rose up in his heart to defend his idolatry. God was testing Balaam's heart to see what was in it and he was failing miserably. God was angry with Balaam because He told him not to go and yet he went anyway. Why did Balaam want to go? He wanted to go because he had been enticed by the rewards for divination. Demonic assignments had found common ground in Balaam's heart.

> "And the ass said unto Balaam, Am not I thine ass, upon which thou hast ridden ever since I was thine unto this day? Was I ever wont to do so unto thee? And he said, nay. Then the Lord opened the eyes of Balaam, and he saw the angel of the Lord standing in the way, and his sword drawn in his hand: and he bowed down his head, and fell flat on his face. And the angel of the Lord said unto him, Wherefore hast

thou smitten thine ass these three times? Behold, I went out to withstand thee, because thy way is *perverse* before me:" (Numbers 22:30-32 Italics added)

The word "perverse" means to deviate from what is considered right. The angel was saying, "I know that I told you that you could go, but your behavior is contrary, it's obstinate. You're not walking according to my ways. You have taken the wrong course." Balaam's idolatry was being exposed. He was unreasonably determined to have his own way. To have one's own way is the idolatry of self-will. Balaam the prophet wanted the "rewards of divination." He wanted all that King Balak had offered:

- Fame

- Money

- Honor

- Power

- Prestige

- Promotion

What was in Balaam's heart that he would murder his own donkey? It was idolatry and God was exposing it. Balaam was a true prophet of God who was deceived and enticed by witchcraft. He was pulled away from the Word of God by the common ground of idolatry and self-will that was in his own heart. All the divination and enticements by King Balak were released at him and he took them into the common ground of his heart. Balaam thought, "I can be somebody. All I have to do is curse these people. After all, what's the big deal? A few little prophetic curses and I can pick up my money. This is my big chance for promotion."

BABYLONIAN DIVINATION

Let's continue to learn how Balaam got off into prophetic error.

> "And the angel of the Lord said to Balaam,
> Go with the men: but only the word that
> I shall speak to thee that thou shalt speak.
> So Balaam went with the princes of Balak."
> (Numbers 22:35)

Again, Balaam could have stopped right here instead of going with the princes of Balak. He could have said, "Lord, forgive me, I heard you the first time and I am turning back." God gave Balaam another chance because he was still proving the prophet's heart.

"And it came to pass on the morrow that Balak took Balaam and brought him up into the high places of Baal, that thence he might see the utmost part of the people." (Numbers 22:41)

"And Balaam said to Balak, 'Build me here seven altars, and prepare me here seven oxen and seven rams.'" (Numbers 23:1)

These are works of Babylonian divination. Balaam was from Pethor that was in the land of Abraham's father called the land of Ur of the Chaldees. This was the heartland of pagan divination and witchcraft in those days. Balaam had seen the practices of Babylonian divination and he knew what would be impressive to King Balak. God never told Balaam to build seven altars and prepare oxen and rams. That was Babylonian divination. (There was only one sacrifice needed for mankind, the Lamb of God that taketh away the sins of the world, Jesus.) Balaam had no intent of seeking God for a revelation or a prophetic word. He wanted to impress the king and pickup his rewards. Those altars were the Babylonian way of conjuring up demons through divination and occult practice. Divination means to tap into the "divine" through sorcery. It is the act or practice of foretelling the future by occult means.

"And Balak did as Balaam had spoken; and Balak and Balaam offered on every altar a bullock and a ram. And Balaam said to Balak, Stand by thy burnt offering, and I will go: peradventure (perhaps) the Lord will come to meet me: and whatsoever he showeth me I will tell thee. And he went to a high place. And God met Balaam: and he said to him, I have prepared seven altars, and I have offered on every altar a bullock and a ram. And the Lord put a

word in Balaam's mouth, and said, Return
to Balak, and thus thou shalt speak."
(Numbers 23:2-5)

Balaam said "perhaps" the Lord will speak to me,
but Balaam never had it in his heart to talk to or
inquire of the Lord. If he had, he would not have said
"perhaps," He would have said, "God is going to speak
to me because I am here on an assignment and God
said go and speak what I tell you." Did Balaam do
that? No! Balaam did not draw aside to get a prophetic
word from the Lord, but, to Balaam's surprise, God
did speak. God did put prophetic revelation in his
mouth. All the while testing this old prophet's heart.
Can you see that? So Balaam came back and spoke
blessings over Israel. Let's read.

"And he returned to him, and, lo, he
stood by his burnt sacrifice, he, and all
the princes of Moab. And he took up his

parable, and said, Balak the king of Moab hath brought me from Aram, out of the mountains of the east, saying, Come, curse me Jacob, and come, defy Israel. How shall I curse, whom God hath not cursed? or how shall I defy, whom the Lord hath not defied? For from the top of the rocks I see him, and from the hills I behold him: lo, the people shall dwell alone, and shall not be reckoned among the nations. Who can count the dust of Jacob, and the number of the fourth part of Israel? Let me die the death of the righteous, and let my last end be like his! And Balak said unto Balaam, What hast thou done to me? I took thee to curse mine enemies, and, behold, thou hast blessed them altogether. And he answered and said, Must I not take heed to speak that which the Lord hath put in my mouth?" (Numbers 23:6-12)

King Balak was furious. He hired Balaam to curse Israel. Instead Balaam blessed them. I think prophetic blessing even surprised Balaam. Balaam wanted the money, the wages of divination. He couldn't believe it himself with words of blessing out of his mouth. What to do? He defended himself by saying, "Didn't I tell you whatever God said, that I would have to speak?" This was all a defense to keep King Balak from killing him.

> "Surely there is no enchantment against Jacob, neither is there any divination against Israel: according to this time it shall be said of Jacob and of Israel, What hath God wrought!" (Numbers 23:23)

Balaam tried to curse the Israelites by tapping into a spirit of divination but he realized that it couldn't be done. He told King Balak, "There is no divination or witchcraft that will curse Israel." So we learn that

God all along the way was proving, trying and testing the idolatry in the heart of His prophet Balaam in an effort to reach him. Prophet, hear me, the Holy Spirit will do the same with you. To keep your heart right before God always check your motives.

DIVINATION AND SEXUAL SIN

Sexual sin, divination, witchcraft and every evil thing is the fruit of Balaam's ministry. He couldn't curse Israel so he taught King Balak something just as hideous.

> "And Israel abode in Shittim, and the people began to commit whoredoms with the daughters of Moab." (Numbers 25:1)

Balaam concluded that it was impossible to curse Israel by divination, yet he had crossed the threshold through idolatry and rebellion. Balaam still wanted the rewards for divination. So, he taught King Balak what would defile Israel. Balaam told King Balak to corrupt the tribes with whoredoms, sexual relations with the daughters of Moab. "We can't curse them through prophetic divination. My solution is to send women into their camps to invite the men to worship with them in their pagan high places. Through sexual sin they will loose the protective covering of God. Tell the women that attend to have sex with them and then you will have accomplished your desire." This was Balaam's sin and it all started with the idolatry in his own heart. Divination always releases sexual sins. That is what Balaam did. Balaam knew that he could entice the men of God through lust. Israel could not be defeated by its enemy's military but they could be defeated through sexual defilement.

SIN OF BALAAM

The great sin of Balaam was not only the merchandising of his prophetic gift and the attempt at cursing Israel, it was teaching the Moabites how to defile God's people. Balaam knew God forbade the intermingling of His people with foreign women (Deuteronomy 7:1-4). He knew that introducing whoredoms (sexual sin) would cause the Israelites to break covenant with God. The word "whoredom" is the Hebrew word zanah, meaning to go a whoring, commit fornication or adultery. By targeting Israel with Moabite whoredoms he ushered in Babylonian paganism and foreign spirits. This unholy mixture, strange fire, was a demonic assignment designed to:

- Turn the people from the Word of God

- Break the covenant between God and Israel

- Defile the bloodline and keep the Messiah (Christ) from being born

God's prophets must avoid the spirit of Balaam at all cost. Because of this great evil, God ended Balaam's ministry and his life. Balaam will forever be remembered as a traitor and fallen prophet. He will forever burn in a tormenting lake of fire.

> "Behold, these caused the children of Israel, through the counsel of Balaam, to commit trespass against the Lord in the matter of Peor, and there was a plague among the congregation of the Lord." (Numbers 31:16)

God broke out against the Israelites who defiled themselves with the women and killed them by plague. God taught Moses to avenge the Israelites on the Midianites and they slew every male including the prophet Balaam.

Thousands of prophets have gone the way of Balaam being seduced by prestige, honor, fame and riches. Never forget this testimony. If this can happen to Balaam it can happen to you too. Throughout your prophetic ministry you will be tested just like Balaam. There is no escaping the temptations. Will you make it? Here is some fatherly counsel, "Keep thy heart with all diligence for out of it are the issues of life" (Proverbs 4:23).

APERÇU

Prophetic ministers must avoid the seducing pull of wealth, honor, prestige and promotion.

The elders of Moab tempted Balaam with rewards, money for divination and money for curses.

Idols are dangerous and deadly

The demonic enticements against Balaam were designed to find any idols in his heart the enemy could use to separate him from God.

The word "perverse" means to deviate from what is considered right.

Balaam tried to curse the Israelites by tapping into a spirit of divination but he realized that it couldn't be done.

Sexual sin, divination, witchcraft and every evil thing is the fruit of Balaam's ministry.

Divination always releases sexual sins.

Balaam will forever be remembered as a traitor and fallen prophet

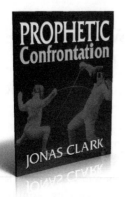

PROPHETIC CONFRONTATION

Spiritual confrontation within prophetic ministry is historic. Examples
include Micaiah, Elijah and Jeremiah.
Micaiah contended with King Ahab's
prophets, Elijah and Jeremiah battled
the prophets of Jezebel and Baal.

ISBN 1-886885-45-1

There are foreign spirits training
prophetic people. Are we about to see
a prophetic showdown within prophetic ministry?

In this pocket-book discover these truths…

- How prophets affect spiritual climates.
- Avoiding prophetic deception.
- Prophetic weapons.
- Six reasons for prophetic confrontation.
- Ten causes of hard spiritual climates.
- And much more...

Order Online at www.JonasClark.com
or call 800.943.6490.

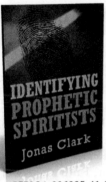

MORE EASY READ POCKET-SIZE BOOKS BY JONAS CLARK

Pocket-Size Books

Entering Prophetic Ministry

Prophecy Without Permission

How Witchcraft Spirits Attack

Seeing What Others Can't

Unlocking Prophetic Imaginations

What To Do When You Feel Like Giving Up

The Weapons Of Your Warfare

Overcoming Dark Imaginations

Healing Rejection and Emotional Abuse

Breaking Christian Witchcraft

Prophetic Confrontations

Unlocking Spiritual Authority

Avoiding Foreign Spirits

How Jezebel Hijacks Prophetic Ministry

How Prophets Fail

Identifying Prophetic Spiritists

**Order Online at www.JonasClark.com
or call 800.943.6490.**

Equipping Resources by Jonas Clark

Books

Extreme Prophetic Studies

Advanced Apostolic Studies

Kingdom Living: How to Activate Your Spiritual Authority

Imaginations: Dare to Win the Battle Against Your Mind

Jezebel, Seducing Goddess of War *(Also Available in Spanish)*

Exposing Spiritual Witchraft

30 Pieces of Silver *(Overcoming Religious Spirits)*

The Apostolic Equipping Dimension

Effective Ministries & Believers

Life After Rejection: God's Path to Emotional Healing

Come Out! A Handbook for the Serious Deliverance Minister

Saboteurs in The Republic: Battling Spiritual Wickedness in High Places

Order Online at www.JonasClark.com or call 800.943.6490.